6/31

- ? Agile vs. Hybrid vs. Waterfa

- ? Who are most consistent champ

ENTERPRISE AGILITY IN HEALTHCARE

Candid Case Studies of Successful Organizational Transformations

ENTERPRISE AGILITY IN
HEALTHCARE

Candid Case Studies of Successful Organizational Transformations

JOHN G. **STENBECK**
PMP, PMI-ACP, CSM, CSP

LAUREN E. **MIX**

A PRODUCTIVITY PRESS BOOK

This book includes references to terms such as PMP®, PgMP®, CAPM®, PMI-SP®, PMI-RMP®, or PMI-ACP®, all of which are registered marks of the Project Management Institute, Inc.

CRC Press
Taylor & Francis Group
6000 Broken Sound Parkway NW, Suite 300
Boca Raton, FL 33487-2742

International Standard Book Number-13: 978-0-367-13817-2 (Hardback)

Visit the Taylor & Francis Web site at
http://www.taylorandfrancis.com

and the CRC Press Web site at
http://www.crcpress.com

Advance Praise

• •

"I enjoyed reading the book. I found it to be a concise, practical, easy to read and useful resource for health care executives and managers who aim to lead their organization with impact."

Manish Kohli MD, MPH, MBA, FHIMSS,
Chair, Global Board of Directors, HIMSS

• •

"A critical read for healthcare organizations struggling with change management. The real-world stories bring the lessons articulated in this read to life."

- Michael J Mirro MD, FACC, FHRS, FAHA, FACP,
Senior VP Parkview Health System Chief Academic – Research Officer,
Past Chair, American College of Cardiology HIT committee

• •

"In this analysis of the Agile journey of two corporate players in the Healthcare space, John and Lauren have hit the ball out of the park! With multiple engagements, I have worked to implement Agile in the dynamic healthcare industry and this guidance would have helped tremendously. When we started Blue Agile, a national group of Blue Cross Blue Shield Agilists, this was what we were searching for -- practical information for fast, simple consumption and application. I recommend this for standard reading at the Academy of Healthcare Management."

- Steve McGee PMP/PMP-ACP/PAHM/CHC/CPHP/CSM/SPC4/ICP,
Senior Managing Consultant, IBM

"I thoroughly enjoyed learning about this alternative type of project management in the health care profession. The team approach and emphasis on a creative trusting environment was very helpful."

- Patricia Gilbreath, MD,
San Diego, CA

. . . .

"If you lack an underlying commitment to 'self-mastery' and growth, the best theory won't help you succeed. The hardest challenge is to be yourself in a world where everyone is trying to make you be somebody else. Desire is the standing point of all achievement. "Enterprise Agility in Healthcare" will set the pathway to a different mindset to improving your leadership role."

- Frank Kelly, Abella,
Director IT Infrastructure Operations, Renown

. . . .

Enterprise Agility in Healthcare explains why agility is vital to organizational survival. It details the critical variables that only executive leaders can address in a way that ensures success. It uses the experiences of two major healthcare organizations to frame the situational context surrounding the variables then explains why and how the leaders in those organizations made choices that proved to be extraordinarily successful … in the real world!

This book focuses on organizational expansion in healthcare. By examining two organizations with similar, yet different, growth experiences, this book demonstrates very successful, very real outcomes while offering key insights into the principles and practices that drove them.

Dedication

Lauren Mix

To my wonderfully supportive husband, Patrick –

Thank you for always being in my corner and cheering me on. Your encouragement makes all the difference. I love you, best friend.

To my beautiful daughter, Mallory-

You are my reason. You are why I do all that I do.
I love you, kiddo.

John Stenbeck

Sitting here, struggling to write this dedication, humbled by the many people who have chosen to bless my life makes my heart overflow with gratitude. Expressing the heartfelt thanks to each of them appropriately is a task more challenging than writing the book. Nonetheless, I trust their generous hearts will allow themto hear how deeply I love them, expressed in this small gesture.

I am compelled to begin this effort with an acknowledgement of the inimitable Lauren Mix, my co-author. Seven years and 7 books ago when we decided to collaborate as author and editor I never could have dreamed of her depth, passion and capability as an agent of transformation, taking my limited prose and making it elegant and accessible in addition to accurate. Her depth was revealed in a new and exciting way when the burning crucible of the Agile Almanac Book 2 seemed certain to overwhelm me and she shifted gears into ghost-writing 3 chapters to push us over the finish line. Finally, she identified the opportunity for the Distilled Insight series and suggested we co-author it. It has been my privilege to work and grow with her. I am certain, and pleased beyond measure, that she will outshine any accomplishment of mine!

I am also deeply indebted to, and grateful for, two friends who have been instrumental in keeping me alive and keeping me focused on the pursuit of significance. John Gates and Rick Morris are both amazingly accomplished thought- and team-leaders who have helped me grow in ways unimagined because of their dedicated, insightful and gracious investment in my life. They continue to challenge, dare and press me to rise to the challenge and potential of their astonishing wisdom. Everyone should be so blessed with at least one such friend in their life, and I am privileged to have both of you as brothers.

I would be remiss to not thank two amazing mentors who came into my life by the accident of us belonging to PMI. The value of John Watson and Michael O'Brochta exceeds even a lifetime of membership dues and volunteer hours. You have been, and always will be, brothers to me.

Last, but certainly not least, my amazing, long-time Cursillo brothers and newly found St. Mary's Men's Group brothers; thank for always cheering me on while lovingly admonishing me to be the man God is calling me to become. Please keep praying for me and know that I love you all!

Of course, none of this would mean anything without the love and joy that JT, Lindsey, Grayson, and Hensley, Michael and Olivia, and Jamie, Bailey and Jason pour into my life. I hope each of you know how much you mean to me and how you inspire me every day to move into the future, embracing it with the expectation of giving and receiving abundantly, without limitation or condition, as you do. Your courage and daring, demonstrated by loving everyone around you, sets a standard for me to pursue. Someday, may I do as well as each of you already do. Love you all...bunches!

Table of Contents

● ●

Welcome

● ●

W elcome to Distilled Insight, the book series dedicated to serving the needs of executives by delivering content-rich, brass-tack information focused on specific, critical issues within their industry at a fast pace because time pressure is the only constant for leaders.

Distilled Insight assumes the reader has the ability to absorb and process information without the authors slowing down or holding their hand. The content has been presented in a way to allow for sectional or complete comprehension out of the respect and understanding of the executive's valuable time.

Distilled Insight does *not* contain cookie-cutter solutions from a fabricated, fictionalized world of what should be. It does contain specific observations and advice from real-world companies who succeeded in doing what you are pondering... *which is why you're reading this!*

About This Book

Enterprise Agility in Healthcare explains why agility is vital to organizational survival. It details the critical variables that only executive leaders can address in a way that ensures success. It uses the experiences of two major healthcare organizations in order to frame the situational context surrounding the variables then explains why and how the leaders in those organizations made choices that proved to be extraordinarily successful ... **in the real world!**

Icons Used in This Book

This book uses the following icons to call your attention to particular information so you can easily spot noteworthy elements when you refer to the content later.

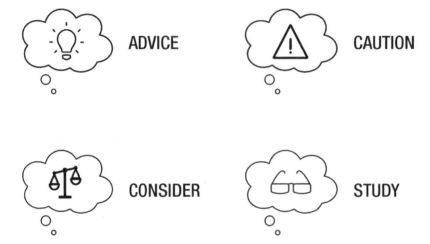

ADVICE

CAUTION

CONSIDER

STUDY

Acknowledgments

· ·

We never could have even written this book without the invaluable input from Jeff Rudisill, Brian Blackwell, Kirk Williams, Michael Elliott, and Kim Moreau at Centra Health or Ron Double and Mark Pierce at Parkview Health. Their successful transformations were the keys to this book being tangible to our readers and their ability to share their experiences so candidly is what will set this book apart from others. Thank you all for taking the time to let us interview you, again and again, and for sharing your stories with us so we can share them in hopes of helping other executives and organizations transform successfully.

Throughout our interviews, a surprising key factor in the success of Centra and Parkview was found in the Change Management role. Thank you to Dan Gamble of Prosci, Inc. and Mark Sasscer of LeadQuest Consulting, Inc for speaking with us in such length and detail about Change Management and your insights into effective executive leadership during organizational transitions. You not only added immense value to the content of this book, you also ignited a "Change Management" fire within us!

Thank you to Hannah Vizza for patiently working with us on the initial design of our cover, logo, and icons. Your creativity and patience created awesome graphics!

We cringe to think where we would be without Tamara Parsons and her amazing graphic design skills. Not only does her ability to take something great and turn it into something even better shock us, it is a catalyst in our success. Thank you for patiently fielding the countless back and forth emails, containing minor tweaks to the design and requests for modifications. Thank you for making our books shine…every single time.

Thank you, Jamison Manion, for giving Lauren that extra keyboard and the virtual introduction to your publisher. We are forever indebted to you.

And finally, we'd like to thank Doug Martin and those who did an advanced read and provided feedback, insight, and praise.

Introduction

● ●

T he existence of universal laws of life and death in organisms is unlikely to surprise healthcare executives and professionals because there is a preeminent priority on saving, extending, and improving human life at the core of everything they do. It may be a surprise to learn there are remarkably similar laws that impact large organizations, especially in times of great change and uncertainty.

The idea of a common, shared framework underlying the success or failure of large, apparently different, organizations trying to thrive in highly-complex industries with dynamically changing growth and contraction cycles seems far-fetched. If, in fact, similar laws *do* exist, and can provide access to the core principles and practices of a quantitative predictive framework for successfully addressing a host of critical, ever-changing questions that cross between the science and art of leadership in healthcare, only a fool would ignore them.

The common challenge shared by healthcare, aerospace, and information-centric industries of every type is the extraordinary complexity and uncertainty driven by the enormous number of individual, yet codependent factors, whether in humans and their cellular functioning, or vehicles and the interaction of materials and environment, requiring leaders and decision-makers at every level to connect, interact, and synthesize vital, fluctuating data, typically via technology-intermediated network structures with varying content and scale. The networks may be obvious, like the organizational structure, while others are more abstract or virtual, like social networks and ecosystems.

 Why do most companies live for only a few years while a select minority manages to avoid an undesirable fate and become powerful, seemingly invulnerable?

 Why does the pace of innovation appear to continuously accelerate and fuel the socioeconomic success of the thriving minority?

 Why do the leaders in vibrant, thriving organizations seem to cultivate an innovation-driven ethos while those destined to fail seem unable to avoid unhealthy conflict and destruction?

Despite healthcare's amazing success in improving the quality and average lifespan of human beings, the maximum lifespan remains unchanged at no more than 125 years. Very few healthcare organizations live for much longer, with most disappearing before reaching one-third of that lifespan.

One core principle is that no system, natural or man-made, can survive without a continuous supply of digestible energy. Accessible resources must be transformed into useful outcomes, healthy tissue, or desirable services in an effective and efficient manner. The second law of thermodynamics declares that whenever energy is transformed, in addition to useful output, it also inevitably produces useless, unintended, disorganized by-products. **The key to success is to improve the ratio of value to waste.**

Regulation and marketplace pressure means that increasing organizational size is nearly unavoidable. In and of itself, size really does matter and cannot be decoupled because scaling is a non-linear variable in the equation of success. Going from a $10 million to $100 million organization is not just different in how much, but actually different in kind when going from $100 million to $1 billion. Beyond the dollar values, the type of facilities, layers and communication needs of the staff, and interactions with suppliers, contractors, partners and regulators all cause a non-linear increase in complexity.

How systems, people, and culture respond as organizational size changes is a challenge and also an opportunity in scaling for any information-centric industry. This book will use the actual, real-world experiences of two, very successful healthcare organizations to provide specific, actionable insights into the principles and practices that provoke success.

Because scaling plays a determinative role in the successful design of everything from airplanes to skyscrapers, its impact on how effective and efficient an organization is remains a continuous challenge. Perhaps understanding scaling is of greater urgency due to the increasingly large and complex structures required for companies, institutions and governments to continuously evolve the complex adaptive systems they have become.

This edition of Distilled Insight focuses on organizational expansion in healthcare. By examining two organizations with similar, yet different growth experiences, this book demonstrates very successful, very real outcomes while offering key insights into the principles and practices that drove them.

The source examples reflect essential principles and practices that harnessed social activity and aligned it with economic productivity, systematically enhancing the value-added "bonus" that is the most important return on scaling from a financial perspective. The benefit of non-linear scaling is similar to the biological advantage seen in the basal metabolic rates of large animals, which are surprisingly more efficient than smaller ones. As size increases, less energy is required to support each gram of tissue, which economists would call a systemic economy of scale.

The terms complex adaptive systems, emergent change, and self-organization have been overused, often without the least rigor, precision or clarity being applied, but resilience as an adaptive organization facing non-linear marketplace dynamics means they are vital to success on the business-side of every organization.

The core principle that no system can survive without a continuous supply of accessible resources being transformed into useful outcomes in an effective and efficient manner is an existential reality in healthcare. The cases shared in this book will show how, due to the application of Agile techniques, "energy was transformed" into useful output while minimizing negative, unintended consequences, both by "accident" and by design.

The eminent physicist, Stephen Hawkins, is reputed to have said, "The next century will be the century of complexity" and that is certainly playing out in the world of healthcare.

Healthcare's Current Climate

Healthcare's current climate is impacted by the reality that every complex system is composed of individual actors, human and not, with collective characteristics not easily predicted from assuming the probable action of the individual variables. In the same way that you are an expression of the countless interactions of the cells of your body, studying the cells will not reveal your consciousness, preferences, or spirit. Similarly, the output, orientation, and culture of healthcare (and all) organizations result from non-linear, independent, and often self-reinforcing feedback mechanisms. These are personified in the interaction between people, infrastructure and environment. As W. Edwards Deming observed, "Any time the majority of the people behave a particular way the majority of the time, the problems are inherent in the system."

The fundamental concept of simplicity, as demonstrated by numerous simulations of complex behavior, is that the best results emerge when the actors can continuously apply simple operating rules to guide the actions of other agents. The simulations have credibly demonstrated that the bewildering dynamics of highly complex organizations perform best when simple, reliable procedures govern the interactions between the actors.

 The rules that guide the collective outcome, with significantly better results than predicted by adding up the sum of the contributions of individual contributors, is called emergent behavior. By creating and applying rules guided by the granularity of the situation, control becomes decentralized and self-organized, and the source of emergent behavior and simplicity develops. The individuals become vested stakeholders, choosing to be cohesive, and the emergent formation is a high-functioning group, ideally adapted to efficiently and effectively transform energy into outcomes. They innovate an ability to adapt and evolve productively in response to the changing internal and external variables of the complex, adaptive environment that is healthcare.

Highly complex, self-sustaining organizations require close alignment and low-friction integration of an enormous number of variables and actors often accomplished in living systems by evolving fractal-like, hierarchal branching networked systems. In order for growth to continue without infinite resources, emergent behavior must provide creative and innovative paradigm shifts before potential organizational collapse occurs. As dire as that sounds recognize that the existential demand for paradigm shifts is fulfilled – by accident or by design – in every large organization experiencing long-term success.

Agility in healthcare is already occurring. This book will showcase proven principles and practices applied in specific initiatives, allowing you to implement techniques selectively.

The Promis nge of Agile

Just like Tesla sedans, FEMA emergency response plans, and Department of Defense technology portfolios, successful healthcare organizations cannot be produced on a large scale without an unavoidably complex supporting structure that must also be adaptive if it is going to thwart the existential threat of a competitive market. That structure integrates the delivery of energy and resources, including capital, to sustain the metabolism of the company. It must also provide seamless information exchange to fuel the innovation and creativity needed for paradigm improvements and shifts.

All companies are complex, adaptive systems, and the *promise* of Agile and Agile Frameworks is the ability to sufficiently address the scaling paradigm with iterative, incremental product and process improvements that create an environment amenable to advances. Successful agility for an organization typically develops in ways that are complementary to existing traditional systems and methods while assimilating new principles and practices that deliver added capabilities and competencies, positioning the organization for periodic bursts or breakthroughs.

The *challenge* of Agile resides in the inherent complexity and uncertainty that surrounds making continuous organizational improvements and embracing the periodic opportunities to shift key paradigms in the midst of marketplace pressure, and sometimes, chaos.

 The most reliably successful strategy basically requires articulating rules that are as simple as possible, aligning to organization defined decision-making granularity, and governing needed interactions with flexibility and consistency. Sophistication is expressed by accommodating the learning and discovery that enable adaptation through realistic evolutionary process change.

Another fundamental concept is that the organization must invest some effort to define standards and expectations around decision-making granularity. For example, the granularity that is possible at the lower level of a sub-project is simply, mathematically not possible at the portfolio level, yet far too many organizations ignore this fact. Doing so violates the Lean principle of avoiding waste and makes continuous process improvement impossible. The solution is to continuously evolve higher-level complexity into finer and finer semiautonomous, interdependent lower-level components that can be developed in an adaptive system and constructed as multiple subsystems. Doing so eliminates misleading, even dangerous, conclusions and decision-making based on faith in false-positive estimating and forecasting. This book will clarify some simple steps for fixing this basic and far too common problem (Part Four – Shared Takeaways, *Pitfall Avoided*).

Agile is a type of agent-based modeling that has great potential. It is becoming more and more apparent that unleashing that potential requires leaders at every level of the organization to participate in this evolution by providing timely feedback with the kind of inputs this alternative framework requires while visibly supporting the process.

Purpose of This Book

- Practical information for fast, simple consumption and application.
- Real examples with real advice showcased for analysis and consideration.
- Discussion starters for your team when evolving your organization.
- Accessible content for selective reading when necessary or preferred.

Distilled Insight books focus on meeting the needs of busy executives by providing robust, practical information that can be consumed quickly and applied immediately. They deliver very high ROI by reducing the time investment required to become functionally literate in the application of principles and best practices *in their industry!*

They also create high value for executives who use them to establish a baseline understanding and a consistent lexicon for the direct reports that make up the core team supporting them.

The content in this book is informed by the deep expertise of the authors as both expert technologists and, perhaps more importantly, practitioners fluent in the language of business *and* the marketplace and regulatory environment where it is conducted. As such, it is intended for business executives and other nontechnical professionals while being completely cogent for the technology leaders within the organization.

By design, it is expected and encouraged that you use it in whatever way best suits your needs and objectives. Read it start to finish to understand and use as a framework for serious discussion with your staff regarding how to become a powerhouse in the ever-changing, evolving and emerging environment that demands reshaping your company to correspond to your markets. Or, select a particular chapter and explore the principles and practices that directly align to a specific challenge your organization or team has encountered.

PART ONE

What Is the Agile Imperative?

● ●

I t is inconceivable that you have not been enticed by the potential or assaulted by the demands of the hype and hysteria surrounding big data, DevOps, Agile, EHR and the transition from ICD-9 to ICD-10 encoding. They are all symptoms of the bigger issues transforming the entire healthcare system. It could be said that all of this unavoidable change is being driven by the Google, Amazon, Facebook (GAF) factor that has radically changed the expectations of your customers, constituents, regulators, and third-party payers. They have all come to expect everything they want, instantaneously, for nothing, and customized to their personal preferences.

The GAF factor is real and only an integrated response will provide the kind of results that are the primary responsibility of the executive leaders of the organization. The *Agile Imperative* is encapsulated in the recognition that the assumption of an economy or marketplace, typically in a state of equilibrium, is a myth that has devastating consequences. The marketplace, now and forever more, is an evolving system with emergent properties impacting underlying interactions between multiple constituent parts that may be complementary, competitive, or both!

Without a serious commitment to enterprise agility, the *Agile Imperative* is an existential threat to your organization. The Agile Imperative is also an invitation to create an organization that reaches beyond surviving and leverages it to thrive!

Professional Response

Responses to the *Agile Imperative* have been varied, but one of the most significant has come from the Project Management Institute (PMI®), the largest voice for the project management profession, with over 850,000 Project Management Professional (PMP®) credential holders and the source of *A Guide to the Project Management Body of Knowledge (PMBOK® Guide), Sixth Edition, Project Management Institute, Inc. 2017.*

. The newest *PMBOK® Guide* has defined a rigorous baseline of principles and practices that can be used to create an organizational strategy and aligned tactical and operational processes that enable an organization to leverage the *Agile Imperative* as an invitation to succeed!

PMI's credibility with your customers, constituents, regulators, third-party payers and auditors is well known. PMI's role as the curator, custodian and guardian of the *PMBOK® Guide,* the source of proven practices, serves your need to avoid false starts and failures. Unlike many of the competing voices hawking their approaches as the only solution to the marketplace challenge, PMI remains arduously committed to a rigorous, research-based method for validating the content in the *PMBOK® Guide.*

An important core concept to recognize is that PMI's effort to define standards means that the principle of hybrid Agile approaches – approaches that integrate the appropriate processes and tools with a "both/and" perspective – is generally superior to the "either/or" approaches being sold in the marketplace by others as the only right solution.

Contrary to the oft stated demand of Agile experts that your transformation must start with Agile training for everyone (*a rather Waterfall approach to*

Agile!), this book shows that starting small and iterating into forward progress while defining a hybrid Agile approach ideally suited to a specific organization and set of marketplace demands is not only viable, but wise.

Marketplace Demand

The proven success of Lean principles, starting with the Toyota Production System, being extended into a host of other industries and services has brought marketplace demand to healthcare in new and continuously more challenging ways.

Despite the high-profile failed launch of HealthCare.gov there are numerous examples of amazing success in mainstream healthcare as well as in closely coupled industries like pharmaceuticals and medical devices.

 This book includes in-depth exploration of two cases that provide interesting differences and complementary insights. One can be characterized as Agile-by-design and the other more as Agile-by-accident. Both were successful.

Vendor Commitment

A somewhat unexpected central principle emerged as it was discovered anew the crucial role vendors must play as trusted advisor, specifying and defining rules for how actors – both human and system – interact and can be adapted to foster optimal decision-making based on data-supported experience and aligned with fundamental principles of patient-centric care.

 Best-in-class healthcare must deal with the incredible challenge of changing the dominant forces that shape current operating behaviors by aligning them with decisions informed by accessible models reflecting the individual capacity of the practitioners and a complete understanding of each patient's needs and capabilities. It requires an ongoing exploration of the emergent practices being used in a specific organization so that a coherent

picture of how to achieve continuous process improvement can occur. This core challenge can be seen as fulfilling the highest standard of Meaningful Use.

Scaling Agile in healthcare will mimic the power laws seen in biological scaling, but with the likelihood of a larger spread around the average because the enterprises are approximately scaled, similar versions of one another. That means that vendor commitment to being a source of creative and practical insight into scaling Agile and how to optimize the network structures specific to healthcare, based on the expertise they have developed from observing continuous feedback mechanisms across a host of client environments, is inherent to their role as a trusted advisor.

To extend the biology analogy, the success of healthcare organizations can be seen as the difference between metabolism and maintenance. Total revenue can be thought of as resources available for metabolic consumption while expenses are life-maintenance costs. To survive, and especially to thrive, the growth of resources, that is the social metabolic rate, must exceed maintenance, and scaling Agile is a promising and proven approach to fostering that resource growth because it leverages the human genius for creating paradigm improvements and shifts.

This book will explore and explain how this important dynamic can be cultivated. It will share specific insights from companies and their leaders, who embraced and successfully engaged the opportunity. The two specific companies were able to manifest significant success while intersecting old systems and paradigms with new technologies and principles. Consequently, they provide an amazing array of promising ideas and pragmatic practices.

We are deeply grateful to both Centra Health and Parkview Health for investing the time to share their story so *you* could be the beneficiary!

PART TWO

Agile By Design: Centra Health

· ·

W
ith Agile methodologies gaining traction in project management it has become clear to many that in order to have continued success or take success to the next level they need to learn how to be more Agile. For some, this realization motivates the cultural shift while others deny the need or resist the migration. This combination was the reception Agile received at Centra Health in 2015 as they prepared to begin the process of selecting a new Electronic Health Record (EHR) vendor.

There are many drivers of Agile transformations. For example, they can be industry driven, vendor requirements, or deficiency repairs. No matter the reasoning, it is important to evaluate current processes to identify what is working, what is *not*, and what may, unknowingly, already be Agile. If an organization approaches an Agile transformation correctly, new habits can be introduced, adopted, and proven successful rather quickly. Good habits can become the new norm faster than expected. This was the case at Centra. Remember the saying, "It only takes three weeks to form a habit."

Centra's General Challenges:

- Increase speed of deliverables or "time-to-market"
- Add new competencies to their Project Management capabilities
- Extend the existing reliable, repeatable process with the new methodologies
- Persuade executives to utilize new (Agile) techniques

Centra's Specific Initiatives:

- Learn Agile Frameworks
- Partner with a new EHR vendor
- Achieve Level 4 on the Gartner Maturity Model

Eliminate Waste

In November 2015, approximately a year into studying Agile Project Management techniques and practices to add depth to the Technology Management Project Management Office (TMPMO) implementation tool box, Centra found themselves at the threshold of the largest project undertaking in organizational history. The need for extending Centra's TMPMO capabilities to include Agile or Hybrid approaches in managing projects was identified as a priority due to the increasing quantity of projects and stakeholder demands for delivering outcomes faster. Additionally, these expectations were also being fostered by vendors of Centra.

Years of project success combined with a year of additional project management education, specifically in Agile, positioned Centra's TMPMO to assume the leadership role in the transition to a new EHR vendor. Embarking on this endeavor armed with an additional methodology in their implementation tool box proved key to the successful outcome.

As the process to select the new EHR vendor progressed, TMPMO Manager, Jeff Rudisill, and his Project Lead, Brian Blackwell, found that more and more software vendors were requesting clients to use an Agile methodology for the implementation process. Feedback received from users had also relayed that Traditional implementations came with too much 'project management overhead' and that users required products to market in much shorter timeframes, and in incremental fashion – not 'big bang'.

In order to address this feedback, the TMPMO had to assess their process to find the deficiencies and opportunities for improvement. Jeff and his team came to the logical conclusion that in order to speed time-to-market they had to evaluate "project management overhead" to determine whether that was where the lag was coming from.

Jeff explained, "Part of what was frustrating our stakeholders the most, I think, was that a lot of discussions occurred during contract planning meetings." He expanded on how information did not always get relayed correctly or promptly to the TMPMO by explaining that Centra's "RFP meetings have a lot of the users involved so the users think the TMPMO knows the discussions they've had, decisions they've made, and information they've shared when the project gets handed off to us, but it hasn't always happened effectively."

 This is not an uncommon issue within an organization. Throughout the different phases of a project, different departments or teams play different roles and are not necessarily part of the whole process. Thus, these departments or teams must rely on each other to collect the necessary information to fulfill their contribution to the project. All too often these departments or teams assume that the others are all privy to the same information and therefore do not relay it until the project hits a deadline or obstacle and the missing information is discovered. Once this occurs, all contributing members must meet to clarify the missing data, unnecessarily delaying the progress of the project and spending overhead time and money by repeating a part of the process. This can be avoided if all members meet upfront or have a repeatable process in place to consistently and thoroughly share information.

Brian reinforced this by stating that when the TMPMO usually becomes involved, "The users feel we are restarting that whole process over, which adds to the overhead from their point of view. It frustrates the user, who thinks

we are delaying, and so we try to expedite the process." This, too, is not uncommon. In order to satisfy the user and compensate for any delays, the process is accelerated, potentially sacrificing quality. Brian added to this saying, "A lot of times, when we expedite the process, we miss things. We miss things just because we don't have the upfront time that everybody else was allowed."

Everyone, at some point, can relate to being assigned a task that was due yesterday. When this is the situation, the rushed fashion of the task alone increases the risk of failure to deliver; whether that means missing a deadline, delivering an unfinished or sub-par product, or running over budget. All parties – from stakeholders to team members to users – should be represented and involved from the onset of a project. It is crucial to include each of these roles throughout the life of the project because each plays a key role in its success. When teams encounter obstacles, such as lack of information or detail, time is wasted if, before being able to gather it, they must bring a party up to speed.

Reduce Time-to-Market

Project Lead, Brian Blackwell, a certified PMI-ACP®, knew that introducing certain Agile practices to their Traditional process could help accelerate time-to-market without sacrificing quality or requiring them to abandon their current, successful process as part of a transformation. Agile skills would positively impact vital areas of the enterprise, such as data warehouse and analytic initiatives, requiring quick deliverable turnaround to the end user. However, Brian was faced with the large, yet very common obstacle of convincing senior management to consider adapting the standard process.

If agreed upon, it would allow project leaders to use proven Agile methodologies, frameworks, and processes and protect Centra from an unsuccessful or costly EHR launch done in a "foreign" methodology. It would also mean that project managers could use multiple project management methodologies tailored to fit the needs of each project in the future. Still, adding Agile and creating hybrid project management capabilities would require education and training in addition to the shift in organizational thinking to leverage the benefits fully.

After years of proven success with a predictive delivery process using consistent, standardized documents designed to meet the project needs of Centra, TMPMO Manager Jeff Rudisill was skeptical that a project could be as successful when executed with Agile as it had with Traditional practices. However, losing internal business to external vendors because the TMPMO lacked an Agile project manager resource forced him to reconsider 32 years of conditioning as a Traditionalist and reassess with an open mind. His decision solidified the cultural evolution towards Agile project management. That decision proved serendipitous when Centra, Brian and Jeff started the project with their new EHR vendor. Empowered with the intent to acknowledge the expectations of faster time-to-market, fostered by both users and vendors, integrating Agile Project Management techniques and practices helped the EHR project in unanticipated ways.

Am I Already Agile?

Before beginning the process of choosing the appropriate EHR vendor, Centra hired Gartner, a world leading research and advisory company, to evaluate all divisions within the TMPMO. This included assessment of toolsets, current methodologies, and communications, and provided insight into their readiness for the EHR implementation.

Overall, Centra's TMPMO received a Level 3 ranking on the Gartner PPM Maturity Model, which was above the industry average of 2.4, suggesting that adopting Agile methodologies might not be as difficult or foreign as they initially thought.

Gartner Level 3 Maturity requires organizations to:

- Practice reasonable resource management – be adequately staffed with talented and capable project managers, matching project demand to resource capacity.

- Understand the difference between a project and program.
- Focus on the whole, not the parts – understand how change in one area affects others.
- Practice collaborative and transparent decision making.
- Establish consistent, reliable, and documented toolsets or delivery mechanisms.
- Assume financial accountability.[1]

Similarly, amongst other things, Agile frameworks require:

- Adequately staffed teams matched with the project needs; preferably dedicated teams.
- "Optimizing the Whole" – understand how change in one area affects others.
- Collaborative and transparent decision making.
- A defined, repeatable process for continuous improvement.
- Accountability on both the individual and team levels.

While Centra had been highly successful with the PMI Traditional waterfall framework for the past 13 years as its formal project implementation methodology, they found it lacked the ability to deliver products to market in a timelier fashion. This evaluation showed exactly how prepared the TMPMO was to implement a new EHR and supported the path towards Agile. As Vice President Chief Information Officer Kim Moreau relayed, "The evaluation was to ensure Centra had an adequate foundation to take on such a large endeavor."

 It surprised the TMPMO to learn how Agile they already were, which is not an uncommon realization. *Take the Am I Agile Already?* quiz at the end of this book to find out how Agile you and your organization are. You may also be surprised at the results!

So, where does an organization with Gartner Maturity Level 3 and vendors and users demanding Agile go? They go Agile…by design!

Take the First Step

Coupling the vendor requests for an Agile or hybrid methodology with the above average maturity level ranking, Centra's TMPMO now had validation that learning and adopting Agile practices was beneficial to the organization, not only to aide in the EHR project, but to reach the next level of maturity. Gartner level 4 requires project leads to manage projects using various methodologies (Traditional, Agile, and hybrid) to deliver new features and functionality to users via a defined Minimum Marketable Feature process. If that's not Agile, we don't know what is!

Agile was the key to success in each and every item on their agenda. Without it, they could not efficiently and effectively deliver the EHR project or advance from Level 3 to Level 4. Yet before they could become more Agile, they had several obstacles to overcome; changing the mindset of executive leadership, learning more of the methodology, and growing the number of certified practitioners.

Preserve and Leverage the Support of Executive Leadership

> *"We have to evolve. We have to change. In order to do that, we have to initiate the change."*
>
> – ED CATMULL, PRESIDENT OF PIXAR AND
> WALT DISNEY ANIMATION STUDIOS

Initial obstacles to introducing Agile practices are similar to any change; resistance to something new and unfamiliar; and the perceived effort and impact to implement the change. The first step towards change is having the conversation with executives to procure their support. Without executive support, a successful adoption of any change is unlikely. It is crucial to an organization undergoing any type of transformation that the support from senior management be visible, reinforced regularly, and fully involved. "The success of an executive leader usually comes as a result of skilled and proper delegation. In the case of change management, the task cannot be delegated," states Dan

Gamble, Account Manager at Prosci, Inc. Research has shown that executives are the preferred messengers of change. Staff members want to learn *why* a change is taking place from the top. They then want to know *how* it impacts them from their direct supervisors. If senior leaders delegate the critical *why* part of a transformation down the organizational chart, or fail to delegate the *how* part, they are effectively damning their own evolution!

For executive readers, the keys to providing full support are to start by:

- Considering the climate of your organization for readiness and need for change.
- Remaining open to allowing your team to integrate new practices into the current process.
- Being prepared to assume an active and interactive role in the transformation.
- Introducing a change management framework, whether it be brought in-house or provided off-site via training and certification.
- Empowering your team to lead the change initiative while visibly championing the transformation.

For readers who support executives, it is important to be fully prepared when suggesting an Agile adoption. You may need to field questions, provide specific examples of successful application, or simply inform on the basics before executives will support the change. For starters:

- Schedule a time to have the conversation with the key decision-makers.
- Select several specific practices to illustrate Agile's benefits.
- Identify when, how, and what group will pilot those practices.
- Explain *why* the Agile practices are being piloted.
- Expect questions and pushback as a normal response.
- Prepare responses and resources that encourage an open-minded exploration.
- Provide a handout with resources for leaders who want more information.

The Centra TMPMO earned the support of their executive leadership over years of successful delivery and project management. When the overall goal of the organization became to advance from Level 3 to Level 4 maturity alongside implementing a new EHR system, Jeff and his team were fortunate to already have executives willing to listen to them about Agile. According to Senior Vice President Chief Operating Officer, Michael Elliott, "Centra's senior management… is not a rubber stamp board. They invest a significant amount of time to learn the process and make the best decisions." And with the TMPMO's history of success, the next step was to allow them to execute the way they saw fit, which they did when tasked with improving the Cerner Revenue Cycle applications that had fallen behind schedule and become critical to the organization. Without an Agile response to getting that project back on track, serious, negative repercussions would have struck the vendor, Cerner, and the company, Centra.

Create a Safe Environment

A great way to introduce Agile into a company's current management technique is to propose the use of one or two Agile practices first. The first Agile practice selected for integration by Centra was the Daily Stand-up meeting since delays in Revenue Cycle progress were being uncovered in their weekly status meeting. Jeff reflected on this saying, "To succeed we – Cerner and Centra – needed to act as a cohesive group; a real team." Vice President Chief Information Officer Kim Moreau echoed this stating, "You can't push each other away during friction. That's when you need each other the most."

Because of the mindset in many organizations that failure is bad many people attempt to hide from any culpability when a project begins to struggle. Agile methodologies preach that people must be allowed to fail so the team can learn from those mistakes, enact continuous improvement and execute more successfully in the future. However, getting people to trust this process can be difficult and a bit scary!

Jeff remarked that, "The first month was certainly rough as far as actually putting everything on the table in a completely transparent way and really understanding how far behind we were as a team. Once we got those discussions underway, we developed a plan that would get us to each iteration point. The team became proud of what they accomplished each day. We found that having Daily Stand-up meetings kept everybody focused on the task at hand, and that focus helped us address barriers on a daily basis. Ultimately, we found that the work got turned around much faster."

 With any change in process, it is reasonable to expect a few bumps in the road. When a project is struggling, it is also reasonable to expect bumps in the road to recovery. If an organization is undergoing change while dealing with a struggling project, it is reasonable to expect some friction. The Daily Stand-up meetings created a situation where vendor and client could work together to solve the problem, which is exactly what Cerner and Centra did. They had to be transparent and communicate effectively in a timely fashion. They had to create an environment where each member felt safe sharing issues or struggles.

One of the main elements of Agile methods is creating that safe environment; one that, as a team, celebrates success and embraces obstacles. Everyone is accountable for the project outcome, not just their part in it. This fosters a cohesive team, which leads to faster, more effective problem solving.

When asked for the main reason why the Cerner Revenue Cycle got turned around so quickly and so dramatically, Michael Elliott explained, "Cerner and Centra had engaged enough to know they were culturally aligned and both investing in the future... The TMPMO worked with Cerner as a partner that they trust." The Agile practice of the Daily Stand-up meeting was a key to achieving and maintaining that relationship.

With the shift in the team's mindset, they began to realize even more positive results in rebounding the Cerner Revenue Cycle program. Jeff added, "We took our daily wins to the program Daily Stand-up and, you know, we announced those. And when you're in the middle of 65 people and get singled out once for recognition as the person who did it yesterday…it's just a really, really good thing for embracing the change to using Agile."

Jeff shared that creating a cohesive environment and implementing a few small, simple Agile practices demonstrated quick, early benefits that helped gain traction in persuading executives. Once executives support the vision and objectives, it is very helpful to have trained change agents to respond to questions and resistance, help encourage a positive understanding, and cultivate cultural support for the change.

Change Management

From the onset, Jeff was able to leverage the endorsements of senior management to motivate the other stakeholders about the ongoing value of moving project management towards Agile, relying upon results that continually and consistently demonstrated measurable improvements.

 An important early insight was the need for serious change management. A recommended practice when implementing any cultural change within an organization is the introduction of a formalized change management framework. This will teach the champions of the change how to combat negativity and resistance with positivity and engagement.

Anyone who has ever worked within an organization knows how difficult it is to go against the grain. It is much easier to maintain familiar practices than to take the time to learn new ones. It is much easier to agree with a nay-sayer than it is to stand up and disagree. Change management guides leaders through the process of handling employees and co-workers who resist change by teaching communication and persuasion skills that allay fears and motivate progress. It teaches leaders important techniques for engaging teams and developing a transparent, cohesive culture.

Change management is a formal skillset essential to maturing a PMO or any other organizational transformation.

Centra selected Prosci, Inc. for this critical role and Project Lead Brian Blackwell was amongst the Centra staff sent to their 3-day certification course. It was also in this seminar where Brian learned about the ADKAR Model® (Figure 1.0) and once he had become a certified change management practitioner, he introduced it to upper management.

Proper change management is a key element to taking the next step in success. "An understanding of change management will serve to help organizational acceptance of Agile through use of the ADKAR model as it provides a research-based standard that is its own leader in the industry," said Jeff of his experience introducing Agile and shifting towards a new set of practices. To further elaborate, Dan Gamble added, "Every 2 years Prosci publishes their research, which has become a standard for change management. The ADKAR model works! It's been proven over and over."

When you create:	You hear:
(A) **Awareness**	"I understand why…"
(D) **Desire**	"I have decided to…"
(K) **Knowledge**	"I know how to…"
(A) **Ability**	"I am able to…"
(R) **Reinforcement**	"I will continue to…"

Figure 1.0 / ©2018 Prosci, Inc., all rights reserved

A Hybrid Approach

Once a Project Manager, CIO, or Team Lead has their "click" moment, where it all starts to make sense, the culture can begin shifting in the right direction. Not being exposed to Agile and all its possibilities prevents that moment from happening. This is where many executives get snagged in successfully transforming the culture or process of their organization – they fail to become involved and immersed in the process and change initiative. Likewise, this is where so many Project Managers get snagged in gaining support from leadership – they fail to present an easily incorporated, new practice to demonstrate potential value.

Coming from Traditional methods, Jeff found it hard to fully embrace Agile methods, which do not map out an entire timeline or budget in detail during the planning phase. "I fought that every day, every week, every step of the way," laughed Jeff when recounting his mindset at the beginning of the process. However, while reading the hybrid chapter (Chapter 8) in Book 1 of the Agile Almanac, Jeff had his "click" moment. He says, "The hybrid approach provided a way to merge the Traditional and Agile methods for comfort and that's when it clicked for me." For Jeff, discovering the ability to tailor a project management approach, using *both* Traditional and Agile methods, made the transition less intimidating and more exciting.

Centra was realizing that the entire Agile methodology did not have to be adopted, but how many CIOs know that? How many stakeholders are versed in all the methodologies of project management enough to know that a hybrid approach is possible? How many of them listen long enough to learn that it is even a possibility? It is the responsibility of the individual who identifies the need for change to educate not only themselves, but also those on the team, top to bottom.

In Centra's case, this has essentially been the role of the TMPMO through classroom and online education. Centra's TMPMO has a strong connection to their regional PMI chapter since Project Lead Brian Blackwell serves as the chapter president for the 2018 term. Brian helped introduce Agile to their group and also acted as a resource for further education. Jeff believes, "The quickest way a project can fail, even if the technology is right, is if the team members cannot do their job or do not understand it." With Jeff's support, Brian has organized forums for conversations with professional PMs from other organizations in the region to share and gather insight.

To begin their TMPMO transformation, Centra selected three Agile practices – Daily Stand-up meetings, Burn-up/Burn-down charts, and Retrospective meetings – to introduce to the organization first. They used a hybrid methodology to best fit current and future initiative requests since the majority of them came with pre-defined deliverables and budgets. Using a hybrid approach also allowed the project leads to continue using defined project plans while delivering products to market in incremental phases instead of the Traditional "big bang" approach.

For any organization, having leadership visibly support Agile is essential to the transition. For Centra, leadership has very visibly embraced Lean principles at the enterprise level for the organization and, since Agile is based on Lean principles, the leadership support remained. It is important to engage stakeholders and sponsors in the process of project management. If they are involved early on, the better their understanding will be on what is expected throughout the process, which leads to stronger support of the process. Conversely, for executives it is crucial to become and stay involved early on for many reasons, such as, what we call, *"The 5 Ms"* (Figure 2.0):

1. **M**otivate the team supporting you.
2. **M**onitor and ensure forward progress.
3. **M**itigate hurdles or obstacles.
4. **M**anage behavioral expectations.
5. **M**odel the desired behaviors of the team.

Whether the support comes easily or not, successful implementation of Agile requires championing and education about how Agile is different from Traditional project management at all levels. A strong leader may internally

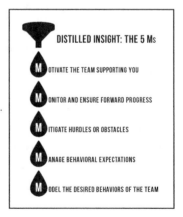

DISTILLED INSIGHT: THE 5 Ms

M OTIVATE THE TEAM SUPPORTING YOU

M ONITOR AND ENSURE FORWARD PROGRESS

M ITIGATE HURDLES OR OBSTACLES

M ANAGE BEHAVIORAL EXPECTATIONS

M ODEL THE DESIRED BEHAVIORS OF THE TEAM

Figure 2.0

determine the need and weigh out the options for change, but to succeed the leader must externally display their support of the evolution.

Be Agile… about Agile

It cannot be emphasized enough that a complete Agile transformation need not take place. Obviously, if a company wants to introduce a new methodology, they need to learn it first. It goes beyond education to application so they know when, why, and how to apply it, or part of it. A hybrid approach can absolutely prove successful and be applied to improve the weaker parts of an existing process.

 Agile methods allow teams to deliver projects in a more expedited fashion. In the case of Centra, the deficiency was not overall. They simply needed to deliver incrementally and faster, and realized that Agile would help make that a reality. Prior to initiating an Agile adoption, the TMPMO had a well-documented, established process of project execution, making it easier to analyze and understand which elements were working and which may need improvement.

One of the mainstays of Agile is having, and using, a well-understood, repeatable process for project execution. Teams with steady delivery of successful projects are the best evidence that a consistent process and toolset are the most effective and efficient way to manage projects. This not only cultivates executive support, but also allows for continuous process improvement, a key in Lean practices. "There is a lot of overhead in Traditional project management, with all the documents and details, when all executives and customers really want are results," says Jeff. In order to speed time-to-market, Centra needed to eliminate waste. Agile does that by default!

Already Agile?

When preparing for any process change, it is wise to analyze existing processes for similarities or ways to bridge the proposed change. This will reduce intimidation and resistance throughout the transition. When team members can relate to a new idea or are familiar with aspects of the new idea, they are far more likely to be open-minded about it. An organization may also find that they are far more Agile than they realized. Many individuals, PMOs and organizations are already using Agile techniques, just not the Agile lexicon.

 Two productive ways of preparing for a change are to examine either the successful or the failing attributes of the existing process and compare them to those in the proposed process. If examining the successful elements, explore the proposed process for similarities that will foster comfort through familiarity. If examining the failing elements, search for aspects that may complement the current, successful parts of the process while simultaneously supplementing the deficiency. Centra employed the first method and discovered that their two most successful process components were easily adapted to Agile – the Project Charter and the Project Plan.

Centra's Traditional Project Charter

Jeff credits the Traditional Project Charter with their success over the past 13 years, stating, "The charter provides budget, deliverables, and timeline approved by senior executives and with that, I feel I have all the information necessary and I know what needs to be done." This aspect of a project cycle is crucial to a project's success, and when an organization has a process of developing and using a Project Charter effectively, they are already ahead of the game. Agile calls the Project Charter the Vision Statement, but, in effect, they serve the same purpose and strongly influence the project outcome.

Project Charters and Vision Statements are both formulated and expressed at a high-level with low granularity. Whether that level is described as the Program or the Roadmap, the principle is to create a value statement aligned to stakeholder expectations that will guide the team as they encounter and resolve development details that could not be anticipated in advance without violating the Lean requirements to avoid waste and apply continuous improvement.

By acknowledging and accepting the unavoidable constraint of non-linear distortion driven by time and size, an Agile PMO can adapt a more light-weight version of the Project Charter as a Vision Statement that will effectively guide the program without dramatically increasing overhead cost. Doing so improves the likelihood of success while reducing the contingent potential cost associated with communication failure that will occur without it.

Centra's Traditional Project Plan

Another successful component of their process is the Project Plan and how they manage it. Centra requires all projects to have an agreed upon Project Plan, which is measured on a weekly basis at a project status meeting. Sounds a lot like a Roadmap, doesn't it? Once they started reviewing the plan daily and stopped looking so far out into the future, they found they more easily adopted this Agile practice. This is another process held in common between Traditional and Agile, although used differently.

Recognizing that daily meetings are commonly applied in Traditional environments as part of the remedy for projects that are in trouble builds a bridge that makes shifting towards or incorporating facets of the new methodology that much easier. If daily meetings can get a troubled project back on track, why not use them to prevent the trouble from occurring in the first place? The Agile contribution has been to specify simple guidelines that keep the meeting focused, lowering the cost of having the meeting, while benefitting from the risk reduction and efficiency gains of having the meeting. The result is a solid positive ROI on the time invested.

With their confidence in particular elements of their existing project management processes and knowledge of individual Agile elements that can supplement their deficiencies, the TMPMO can focus more on educating themselves in additional Agile practices that can commingle with the existing, successful techniques.

How to Succeed With Agile

Centra TMPMO's current departmental strategy is to reduce technology implementation times using Agile methodologies, develop a repeatable process, and create a reusable infrastructure. As stated earlier, an organization does not need to make a complete transformation to Agile project management. A hybrid approach, of both Traditional and Agile practices, may suit the project teams better. Mixing techniques can be a more comfortable, and therefore more welcomed, way to ease into a new method of managing projects.

 In order to use a hybrid approach, collaborative and transparent decision-making needs to occur. The team must consider things such as current communication flow, roadblock identification and resolution, and task delegation and accountability. Feedback from all team members should be welcomed and encouraged. It is helpful to write down what is currently working and what is not. Brainstorm as a team, discussing different Agile solutions to Traditional problems. Once these have been determined, apply them to the existing process.

"Great things in business are never done by one person. They're done by a team of people."

- STEVE JOBS

Cerner's Revenue Cycle implementation, comprised of 6 projects and responsible for revenue, was only 32% built when the TMPMO was asked to engage. The TMPMO requested that a project plan be created and agreed upon, which was done in the safe environment described earlier, and they then decided to incorporate the Daily Stand-up meeting into their existing process. Roughly three weeks after implementing the Daily Stand-up, explaining how it worked and practicing the ceremony, the team started realizing the benefits. According to Jeff, "Life was injected into the program." In fact, the results were so invigorating, that roughly 90 days after the teams started holding Daily Stand-ups, they were 100% built.

Merely holding Daily Stand-up meetings sounds too simple to have produced such an increase in development progress, doesn't it? How did such a minor process change produce such major results?

 Jeff and his team found that the Daily Stand-up narrowed their focus onto the day-to-day needs rather than looking too far ahead, and the results were almost immediate. By concentrating only one interval ahead, daily rather than weekly, and focusing on the 3 points of the Daily Stand-up – What work happened yesterday? What work is happening today? What is hindering the work? – Centra increased individual accountability and productivity, which directly correlated to increased individual ownership over the team's successes and failures. Involving the stakeholders in their Daily Stand-ups expedited their delivery times by identifying and resolving roadblocks sooner and collaboratively. This involvement of executives and other stakeholders also motivated the team by illustrating the importance of their progress and reinforced the team culture from "top to bottom."

Basically, the introduction of the Daily Stand-up:

- Narrowed individual and team focus onto the day-to-day needs.
- Allowed the team to identify and resolve obstacles before they impeded project progress.
- Increased transparency by discussing individual team member task progress.
- Increased accountability and ownership over successes and failures.
- Fostered and encouraged a team environment, where members realized the impact of their behavior.
- Reinforced the importance of their progress by involving the stakeholders.
- Reduced waste by shortening the length of the meeting in two ways: the 3-pronged question of progress and simply standing rather than sitting.

With this single Agile practice proving successful, the team had validation that the TMPMO was able to evolve rather painlessly. Michael remarked, "Anyone could walk into any project within the organization and realize the effectiveness of its management. If they examined it closely, they'd see that the reason was due to the involvement of the TMPMO…and that's powerful."

The TMPMO can now progress towards delivering products to market with an accelerated process by learning and incorporating more Agile practices. Being knowledgeable in both Agile and Traditional methods allows a PMO to implement project initiatives via multiple methodology options based on a project's need. The most crucial aspect of learning and experiencing Agile is that it becomes an option for implementation. A project manager only stands to benefit from having additional tools to manage projects.

Adding Agile to a PMO's toolbox will provide another project framework for use, where appropriate, to shorten the time and cost from concept to delivery of project deliverables without sacrificing quality. Very importantly, project leaders will also be able to identify which projects will benefit from a specific framework. Having the ability to articulate to stakeholders at project initiation why a specific framework should be used to manage a specific project will improve stakeholder decision-making; a primary objective of any PMO.

Training and Certifying Leads in Agile

Similar to the credibility of having a Professional Project Manager (PMP®) credential, as an organization evolves into one that has multiple methodologies to draw from based on the needs of the project the next natural step would be for project managers and leads to get certified in Agile. Doing so will strengthen the organizations ability to consistently execute projects effectively and efficiently. (We recommend the PMI Agile Certified Practitioner (PMI-ACP®) for serious consideration.)

When preparing for certification, candidates best suited to manage in a servant leadership role should be selected, the cost evaluated, and timing planned. The benefits of having a PMI-ACP® certified Project Manager far outweigh the minor cost and scheduling adjustments to do so. However, it is worth noting that these are elements to consider when taking this step in your transformation.

If asked, Jeff Rudisill and Brian Blackwell would likely say that they enabled a successful cultural shift and are well on their way to achieving the next level of PMO maturity. Centra continues to employ a hybrid approach to their monthly average of 70 project initiatives in addition to their EHR implementation. With an aggressive timeline and full agenda, the only way to accomplish their goals is with the use of Agile methodologies... by design.

PART THREE

Agile By Accident: Parkview Health

• •

A s the competitive landscape continues to demand faster time-to-market delivery, companies are responding by adopting new project and product management techniques that leverage incremental development. In Centra's case, they explored Agile, selected a few of its elements to supplement their Traditional process, found a hybrid solution that worked for them then executed their objectives using those new hybrid methods. For other companies, it can be less calculated and intentional, but no less successful.

In February of 2011 Parkview Health needed a booster for their current management style to accelerate their entire process. With no goal to do anything other than revamp their current process, they developed new management techniques and practices and successfully navigated through the obstacles to their objective; facilitating fast paced, company-wide growth seamlessly. Parkview did not set out to adopt a particular methodology or even pieces of one. They simply pursued an intelligent strategy for success and transitioned into Agile by accident!

Parkview's General Challenges:

- Optimize their record management system across all platforms of care.
- Reduce the amount of time during the decision making process.
- Form a cohesive approach to administering change throughout the organization.

Parkview's Specific Initiatives:

- Convert the 21 existing record management solutions to one EHR system that satisfies Meaningful Use requirements and benefits from ARRA incentives.
- Select the new EHR vendor and begin building the system in a compressed timeframe.
- Develop a repeatable process to ensure continued growth and success.

The atmosphere in 2010 of Parkview Health, a non-profit community healthcare system, was one on the verge of growth. As a medium-sized health system with approximately 200 doctors, utilizing 21 different medical record and patient/practice management systems, it became clear that they needed to find a vendor that could, singularly and electronically, encompass their needs and growth potential. They also faced the new Meaningful Use (MU) requirements included in the American Reinvestment and Recovery Act (ARRA) , making it difficult to be compliant using any of their current platforms.

In February of 2011, the Board of Directors gave Chief Information Officer (CIO) Ron Double and Chief Medical Information Officer (CMIO) Dr. Mark Pierce the direction to find a new EHR that could achieve Meaningful Use and satisfy the ARRA requirements. Because of ARRA and MU, many other health systems were also in the process of converting their record management systems to meet these new requirements. This meant that numerous EHR vendors would be marketing themselves for these opportunities. Parkview saw this as their opportunity to take the first step in accelerating their evolution.

Eliminate Waste

Parkview set an aggressive goal for their EHR conversion. They not only wanted to begin contracting with the new vendor in June and converting within 16 months, but also aimed for full completion within 3 years when the industry standard at the time was 5 years. To meet these incredibly high aspirations, they had to find a way to accelerate their process and they had to find it fast. The realization had occurred that creative adjustments to standard project management methods to meet organizational and regulatory requirements, defined timelines, and limited funding were more than necessary, they were inevitable.

With so many vendors offering various solutions to electronic record management, the thought of beginning the vetting process was daunting. Coupled with the compressed timeframe for execution, it was overwhelming. This was the first step down the path of a huge endeavor for Parkview, and specifically for CIO Ron Double and CMIO Dr. Mark Pierce.

Vendor Selection

In order to quickly narrow down the field of EHR vendors, Ron and Mark decided to "short change" the request for proposal (RFP) process. Instead of asking each vendor to tailor their RFP response to Parkview's needs, "We asked each vendor to provide a standard RFP response for an integrated network system," said Ron. By not requiring RFP response customization, Ron and Mark compacted the RFP response time, buying more time for their own process. This also produced generic responses, which was exactly what they wanted as it allowed for faster feature comparison. The amount of time that was saved due to this decision was so exceptional that Ron and Mark took this "Short Changed RFP Process" and normalized it throughout the company afterwards.

It is worth noting that this is the same concept as using Rough Order of Magnitude (ROM) estimates in Agile practices. There is no reason to add unnecessary levels of detail to something that is uncertain, unable to be validated at that

time, or not guaranteed to remain in the project. (More on this in Part Four – Shared Takeaways, *Pitfall Avoided*). For instance, if (hypothetically) 10 EHR vendors each spent 10 business days compiling their customized response to and faster, and realized that Agile would help make that a Parkview's RFP rather than 5 days composing a response focused on the features of their EHR system, which they likely already have together for marketing purposes, Ron and Mark will spend one full week of time waiting for details not pertinent to their evaluation. Also, out of the 10 vendors, ultimately only one would be awarded the contract, making the efforts of the other nine fruitless and superfluous.

It is also important to point out that this is a Lean practice of eliminating waste. There is no need for each potential vendor to spend time directing responses to Parkview's specific needs at this juncture in the process. It is time wasted for the vendor, who may not win the job. It is time wasted for the client, Parkview, who has to wait for the responses to be customized then evaluate each RFP's contents that will likely contain solutions and projected capabilities based on varying assumptions of Parkview's anticipated growth.

Instead, having each RFP generically map out the vendor's current abilities on an integrated network system and projected future scenarios, using common, non-specific language makes it much easier to compare them while saving costs for all parties. This approach also motivated the vendors because, as Mark pointed out, "The vendors likely were relieved at the lack of customization and realized the sale would happen quicker because of it."

In order to maintain the desired pace without sacrificing the quality of the vetting process, the Director of the Operational PMO and Process Improvement Group, Kathy Rhodes-Wright, was transitioned into the role of Project Director on the EHR project, taking point on day-to-day progress (much like a Scrum Master). This proved crucial to organization and forward progress in this new approach. Parkview was able to narrow their search options rather efficiently by coupling these concepts.

In fact, the "Short Changed RFP Process" and the role of Project Director were both normalized, with Kathy leading the first year of implementation until she moved on and Brenda White, the Information Systems Director, was passed the baton and seamlessly continued the new process.

Once they narrowed the selection to five EHR vendors vying for their business, Ron and Mark invited each to present their system directly to Parkview's teams and decision makers. In a rented lecture hall, with approximately 200 physicians and 400 leaders in attendance, the vendors presented their systems and capabilities within strict timeframes and guidelines provided by Ron and Mark. Vendors were directed to focus their presentations only on their current abilities and not to speculate on their future abilities. Mark expanded on that saying that looking too far into the future "allows too much room for misunderstandings and empty promises. Parkview just wanted to work in the moment; what the moment will be like when we execute because accountability is important and the future is an unknown."

 This approach is another example of the Lean practice of waste elimination. Projections about future capabilities would add no value to Parkview's assessment because the future is unknown. It also ensured that each leader participated in the process since "getting that many leaders to read a response to an RFP on their own is next to impossible," stated Ron. He then elaborated on involving the number of physicians and leaders they had, remarking that it, "allowed Parkview to get the information across the board without hampering time. This created buy-in and support within the team and since so many people were involved in the decision making process, there was less pushback during execution."

Including so many physicians and leaders in the vetting process "guaranteed everyone got the same message and opportunity to participate. Behaviorally, it played well into the change management objectives," explained Mark. Many studies have been performed on the influences of behavior within organizations and they all point to "monkey-see, monkey-do."

Parkview was able to quickly sift through what system solutions each vendor could offer by carrying out the evaluations in an interactive, generic, factual manner. Conversely, it also facilitated faster elimination of those who could not provide what Parkview needed. At the end of the demonstrations, Parkview invited only two vendors, Cerner and Epic Systems, back for a more thorough review, involving presentations targeted to each user group – such as surgery, revenue, and in-patient care. This engaged physicians and leaders by delivering a complete, integrated plan of care, giving Ron and Mark a support platform for decision making. This selection process also enabled the evaluation of each vendor's whole cost and process from all perspectives.

 The inclusion of so many physicians and leaders in the interactive RFP presentation phase and more thorough, "smaller sessions" phase is aligned with Agile practices in the sense that Ron and Mark approached the entire evaluation process more as Scrum Masters than as Traditional Project Managers. Rather than making the decision without team feedback, they assumed a more lateral role and relinquished control to gather input before guiding the process forward. By involving the users of the system in the selection process, Ron and Mark fostered team ownership of the new EHR system.

Often times, organizations will have senior management select such business elements without consulting those within the organization who will use it and be affected by it on a daily basis. The participation of users in the selection process cultivates a team environment where each member feels valued. However, it is important not to confuse group participation with delegation. Just as it is less effective for leaders to make decisions *for* the team, it is equally ineffective for them to delegate responsibility and "walk away". Parkview completed this process successfully because the leaders (Ron and Mark) empowered others on the team to participate and collaborate *with them* in the decision-making process, but maintained personal responsibility for success.

Ultimately, Parkview selected Epic Systems as their new EHR vendor because they felt Epic "had the complete package to manage our many mergers and acquisitions while maintaining strong records and a continuum of care. It was important that we created a single story of patient care and we felt Epic could best provide that," said Ron. The next step was to agree on contract terms. As many executives, leaders, and project managers know all too well, contract negotiations can be a very time-consuming, lengthy process. In order to speed this part of the process up, more waste needed to be eliminated.

Reduce Time-to-Market

Think about a contract negotiation, specifically for something as integral and sensitive as medical record management. Whether you have or will never be involved with something like this, it does not take much experience, in any industry, to know that this is a huge undertaking for an organization. Likewise, it does not take much experience, in any industry, to know that any huge undertaking likely involves many different departments – from Legal to HR – especially when negotiating contractual terms. Reviewing and deliberating between an organization's departments may take time, but doing so with a vendor takes even more. Thus, Ron and Mark's next obstacle became how to eliminate waste from, what was surely going to be, a lengthy process.

 In today's business environment, practically everything is discussed via email. As beneficial as having things in writing is, waiting for responses can be time-consuming, causing unnecessary delays. Often times it is not even the effort required to respond to an emailed inquiry that causes the slow reply. Usually, it is the case that an email is received then placed on the "to-do list" with several other tasks and emails only to be passed over for other items on the recipient's agenda. Several days pass before the email is even acknowledged then several more before the response is emailed

back even though the overall effort to respond took less than an hour! To avoid this situation, Ron and Mark arranged a dedicated time-block for all necessary Parkview and Epic representatives to meet *face-to-face* in a conference room to review and negotiate contract terms and conditions.

"Any time there are attorneys locked in room, that's a good start," joked Mark. Starting on the first of June Parkview and Epic representatives – and their attorneys – met in a conference room for three consecutive days and emerged with 90% of contract negotiations complete. This fast pace was possible because the decision-makers on both sides were physically present and engaged in the process, without interference from other tasks. There was no need to email questions or comments back and forth as they could simply have a dialogue, whether amongst themselves or with each other.

 This is directly in line with the Agile recommendation of colocation. The physical colocation of the decision-makers aided the prompt resolution of obstacles and acquisition of answers and approvals by eliminating the time between emails. When teams are colocated, both verbal and non-verbal cues can be used to clarify, answer, or define.

Another element of their success with this part of their process was due to the collaborative partnership that Parkview and Epic had created during the vetting period. Mark relayed, "Both Epic and Parkview wanted success for the other. Epic took the time, just as Parkview had, to ensure the partnership would be a good fit. Parkview almost felt *courted* by Epic prior to signing a contract." A large contributor to the accelerated pace was the solid relationship between vendor and client that was nurtured by leaders on both sides in order to realize a successful outcome.

Once the heavy lifting had been completed in those 3 days spent in the conference room, the entire contract was finalized over the following two weeks and Parkview was ready to begin building their Epic EHR.

After accomplishing their first milestone – contracting with a new EHR vendor by June – Parkview now had to assemble and certify a team of 70 people to perform the build. The next certification session was being offered in August, which meant that the team had to be organized and registered by July 7th. Where to begin, right?

Partner with an SME

Screening, assembling, and certifying a team of 70 developers had the potential to be a very complex problem. To reduce training challenges and ease the transition, Ron and Mark decided "to staff the team using internal domain experts and train on the [Epic] technology rather than the reverse." Once again, they unknowingly employed another Agile technique – using subject matter experts (SMEs) for their team. However, their challenge was not whether they *had* domain experts. It was how to expedite evaluating, interviewing, and registering only 70 of the 130 applicants for the team within three weeks' time.

To do so, CIO Ron Double and CMIO Dr. Mark Pierce found themselves, once again, in a conference room with the other decision makers – the Chief Operating Officer of Physicians' Group (COO), the Chief Nursing Officer (CNO), the Chief Medical Officer (CMO), Human Resources (HR), the Project Director, and the Chief Financial Officer (CFO) – this time interviewing candidates. Over the course of 2 weeks, they selected the 70 people who were registered to be certified in August and begin building in November. The Agile process had proved itself successful again!

Change Management

In order to achieve their goal of completing their EHR system conversion within 3 years, Ron and Mark continued to revamp more of their project management methods, which included, amongst other things, the successful, yet unintentional, implementation of more Agile techniques.

Because an entirely new EHR system is a major overhaul to any health organization, Ron and Mark saw a need for change management. They engaged

LeadQuest Consulting, Inc., a change management firm providing change agent skillset training and guidance on how to execute their change plan as effectively as possible. By doing so, they enacted a culture change far beyond their initial scope. In fact, Mark Sasscer, President of LeadQuest, recalled, "When we started [with Parkview] their goal wasn't a total organizational culture change. They simply became really passionate about adopting this new mentality."

 Whenever any large change is occurring within an organization there are several factors – the type of change, who or what department is initiating the change, and the need for the change – that influence whether the cultural adoption occurs smoothly or in a forced manner. There is always an element of resistance simply due to the fact that with change comes the unfamiliar, which usually translates to additional work, at least upfront. In the beginning stages of any change, generally before its specifics have been announced, negativity surrounding the idea can brew and spread through a company like wildfire, creating the need for change agents.

There are two main ways to pioneer change. One is to use people within the organization who have authority over others to influence the adoption. This is the most common method when an organization effects change. It usually comes in the form of a company-wide email, detailing the change, the reasons for it, and new procedures accompanying it. The email is informative, positive, and contains an expression of gratitude-in-advance for everyone promptly embracing the change. It is an announcement or, in other words, a directive from upper management. Reading between the lines, it says, "If you want to keep your job, here's the way to do it." This method usually elicits compliance, but not engagement, which is far more desirable.

Parkview took the other, less common way to effect change and selected individuals within their organization who play an active, visible role in daily operations and trained them to be change agents. They named the group the "E.P.I.C. Physicians Champions" team, which stood for Enabling Parkview's

Integrated Care and was comprised of physicians who were taught how to address detrimental attitudes and overcome negative opinions of change that can impede the success of a transformation. According to Sasscer, "the team quickly embraced this empowerment…and came to the realization that many of the concepts were common sense yet seldom put into common practice." The change champion team learned how to recognize pushback, no matter how subtle, and work through any negativity, allaying fears and concerns while promoting enthusiasm and cooperation.

This approach proved to be a successful investment of both time and money because it addressed resistance before it could fester and spread while simultaneously creating a transparent environment where individuals felt involved in the process rather than mandated to it. According to both Ron and Mark, the role of change management and the techniques learned and applied were crucial to successfully completing the EHR conversion. Mark elaborated that, "The key to successful change is a large group of executives or change champions who can handle the conversation when someone starts to bad mouth the system. We had that."

 The choice to engage change champions paralleled the Agile commitment to a mindset where transparent communication can occur in an environment of personal safety so that real risks are identified and perceived, but false-positive risks are eliminated. It was another example of real leadership aligning "by accident" with core Agile principles.

In order to create this safe environment, Parkview attended multiple retreats and workshops hosted by LeadQuest where they were introduced to Lead-Quest's 10 Principles "in direct context with their Epic implementation, with focus on the application of the principles and doing real work, not just discussing theories," stated Sasscer. The focus on actual examples and not just hypothetical situations is as key to achieving the desired results as team members being open to feedback and personal growth opportunities.

Sasscer said, "High performance equals desired results *plus* desired behaviors. Some executives may get results, but they get them by using the wrong behaviors…Most organizations only deal with behaviors when there's a problem and don't realize how much behavior influences the culture of an organization." Mark and Ron, in working with LeadQuest, were able to take their training and combine it with the passion to truly embrace a culture change and help those around them do the same. "They created a mini-culture of accountability and mutual respect…and leveraged that to connect the purpose of the change to each team member," recalled Sasscer. And when the behavior of a team member went astray, they met the challenge head on and in person.

ROADBLOCK ALONG THE WAY

The decision to utilize change management and create a team of change champions showed one of the largest returns on investment during the rollout process. All 752 Parkview staff members were required to be trained and certified to use the new EHR system. Among this group all but one had been trained prior to the launch of the Epic system, which replaced all paper orders. Ron and Mark had been very clear about this requirement during the entire implementation process. They were also prepared for resistance because of their change management training.

One Friday evening, Mark received a phone call that the on-call physician for a pediatric case was not using the EHR system and was, instead, still writing paper orders. When the staff informed the physician that this was not protocol, he became angry and even more resistant to the EHR change. Uncommon to the "normal" leadership response, Mark left a dinner engagement and physically went to the hospital to speak with this physician and reiterate the expectations of Parkview providers. Mark also took the time to enter each order for the patient into the system with this doctor. Once the immediate needs of the patient and staff were addressed, Mark and the CMO met with the physician – over that weekend – to ensure he understood the expectations Mark re-communicated and confirmed the physician wished to remain practicing at Parkview.

Monday morning at 6:00, the doctor registered for training and certification to continue practicing. The roadblock, negativity, and resistance had been hurdled with a few simple, straightforward conversations that occurred with the right leaders reacting in a prompt timeframe. Not only were the change management tools effective, but Mark and the CMO's commitment to the success of the EHR solidified that leadership supported the team's approach and showed that everyone was involved. By responding to this resistance in the manner they did, Parkview managed to have all 752 providers trained and certified on the EHR system in record time.

● ●

Preserve and Leverage the Support of Executive Leadership

Utilizing effective change management techniques was only one element of Parkview's success, however. When executing an initiative as complex as a system conversion, the project management methodology can make or break the outcome. In addition to Parkview operating with over 20 different record management systems, they lacked a uniform project management process. Without a formalized project management process, they had no prior need for professional project managers and, therefore, had very few on staff. In order for the Epic conversion to occur at all, let alone successfully, Ron and Mark assigned a process expert, with knowledge of project management practices, to outline and ensure the teams followed the same methodology and stayed within guidelines. Sounds a lot like an Agile coach, doesn't it?

To assist with and oversee this process, Ron and Mark created the "E.P.I.C. Ops" team, comprised of themselves and the Project Director, COO, CFO, CNO, and CMO and made it responsible for day-to-day decisions. They also began holding weekly Stand-up meetings with the teams followed by a 4-hour "After Meeting" – another meeting common in Agile – for the Epic Ops team to assess hurdles, resolve obstacles and facilitate consistent forward progress. Additionally, they leveraged their existing quarterly Leadership Development Institute (LDI) meeting where, in addition to discussing safety, quality, growth, and financial accomplishments and goals in general, senior management and guest speakers would focus on the importance of the Epic conversion, emphasizing their commitment and support to its successful outcome.

This engagement and involvement of stakeholders promoted positivity about the change and reinforced the message of a transparent team environment with all members, top to bottom, working together towards the same goal. This proved to be, "one huge key to their success. The top down support – from Board members and the CEO – generated commitment to the project," remarked Ron about the involvement and message of executives at the quarterly meetings.

 It is very important to have the expressed support of leadership during times of significant change. It is equally important to develop processes and procedures that can be duplicated successfully for future projects. Recognize that no one can continuously improve a process that does not exist. Therefore, establishing repeatable guidelines should be as much of a priority to any organization adopting new practices or methods as assigning the role to manage them.

It is also worth noting that the three meetings introduced to the Epic project were vehicles of continuous improvement. Each served a purpose to ensure its process improved along the way. This is yet another component of Lean practices and Agile methods and should be part of any new procedures.

Incremental Delivery

Seven months after beginning the Epic build, Parkview went live with five practices, containing 60 physicians. As they continued rolling out in waves until each practice was live, their quarterly meetings became equally effective in further illustrating the progress of the Epic conversion to the stakeholders. It is not very surprising that incremental delivery was successful. After all, it is one of the cornerstones of Agile practices! Delivering a product or system in phases is not a new concept nor is it blatantly Agile. Hence, Ron and Mark, once again, accidentally embraced another Agile practice and, once again, it resulted in success.

The Result of the Transformation

Over the course of two years, Parkview completed their Epic conversion, successfully transforming their organization from a mix of disparate systems to utilizing one EHR system that not only received the ARRA incentives but satisfied Meaningful Use. However, Parkview actually accomplished quite a bit more in that time.

Concurrent with their Epic conversion, Parkview was in the process of serious growth. They added 250 additional physicians and were building both a new regional medical center and community hospital. In just over 2 years, Parkview had transformed their organization to one EHR system, added a new regional medical center and a new community hospital, and doubled their physician staff while only going 0.2% over budget. If that's not efficient, we don't know what is! And they could not have done it, at least not with the same results, without (accidentally) using Agile!

Since going live with Epic, a formalized project management process has been established, more individuals have been familiarized with the PMBOK® Guide, and Agile practices are being explored to develop a hybrid approach to project management. "The whole process over the past 2 years has been evolutionary, almost revolutionary," commented Mark when referring to the transformation at Parkview.

The Retrospective

"The mark of a good action is that it appears inevitable in retrospect."

– ROBERT LOUIS STEVENSON

During the major overhaul at Parkview Health, many leaders were energized and excited by the evolution and faster pace, looking forward to its outcome. There were also many who were scared of it, pushing back against its progression. Change management was the answer to this conflict. It trained leaders to help those who were afraid to see the potential and success of the new system and culture.

Similarly, many project management methods were productive and beneficial, effecting successful delivery. There were also some that were impractical and inefficient, extending timeframes. Agile was the answer to this conflict. By incorporating Agile techniques, despite being accidental, Parkview was able to maintain the components that worked while supplementing them with new methods that complemented yet expedited their existing process. "One of the challenges with the *PMBOK® Guide* in the past is that it seemed to be inflexible. The Agile component is crucial to the *PMBOK® Guide* because the hybrid approach is very appealing," stated Ron.

The future for Parkview is one of growth. Although their project management is still maturing, "where it is, it's Agile," says Mark. He then continued, "Parkview is starting to realize that, in today's world, we have to be more nimble, more Agile. If you look back at that time of great change in Parkview history and how successful it was, it's only a matter of time before the lightbulb goes off and we realize that the methodology is what drove that. Maybe then we can take the steps to *purposefully* move towards Agile project management across the organization."

Taking the first steps always seem like they are the hardest part of an Agile or hybrid adoption, but, as in the case of Parkview, many teams within organization are already using Agile project management methodology practices and techniques. They just aren't using the Agile lexicon.

That is very common so we invite you to take the **Am I Agile Already** quiz at the end of this book to see just how Agile you already are!

PART FOUR

Shared Takeaways

• •

Two Common Denominators

T hroughout the process of dissecting both Centra and Parkview's initiatives we noticed that change management (CM) was extremely crucial to the successful outcome of each. Similar to their contrasting paths to Agile, Centra and Parkview took very different approaches to change management. Jeff and Brian from Centra opted for Prosci's off-site, intense 3-day deep dive certification course while Ron and Mark from Parkview partnered with LeadQuest Consulting Inc. and brought their training and coaching in-house. Brian became a certified change management practitioner, learning the methodology and bringing the toolset back to teach others in Centra to support execution. Ron and Mark and the E.P.I.C. Ops team worked closely with LeadQuest throughout their transformation, being coached along the way. Even though the situations and approaches were different, both Centra and Parkview benefitted from the way that their leaders acted on the fundamental requirement for change management and, it became loud and clear that without it a successful transformation was out of reach.

Change Management and Executive Involvement

There is no industry in the world that needs change management more than healthcare, specifically in America. It is constantly being bombarded by changes. Change collisions, change fatigue, and change saturation are all very realistic so it is crucial to any organization to properly manage changes so they don't overrun each other and exhaust the staff. In the cases discussed in this book, both Centra and Parkview understood that change is a process and people need to go through the whole process to accept the change in order for it to succeed. The unavoidably-human probability of negative reactions as a common consequence had to be seen not as separate, unique problems but as part of the entity – the ecosystem – where an explicit regard for each person and role demonstrated by an appropriate investment in managing systemic expectations and interpersonal relationships would have powerful consequences to the bigger picture.

For executives in healthcare, the hyper-complex environment is similar to other large companies with thousands of employees and contractors who struggle to access the benefits of Agile. What makes healthcare different are the life-altering consequences included in so many decisions being made in the midst of all the other complexity. That means every leader in the c-suite, and the cohort that supports them, must accept that change is hard and apply systems thinking to their domain. Change is hard for them, personally, their team, and everyone in the organization.

To unleash culture change executives and leaders must recognize the critical, unavoidable human dimension and make a serious, visible commitment to optimizing it. The underlying principles that determine behavior in highly complex systems are a network where the dynamics and structure are inextricably linked and must be considered if their salient properties are to be understood. The inertia of the status quo and the potential risk of someone acting badly is common – and commonly ignored – when transformations are undertaken leading to many negative consequences.

Think of change management as organizational transformation insurance. You don't take out car insurance after you've had an accident! The same should be true for learning a formal change management process. Dan Gamble of Prosci wisely stated, "Change management is the insurance against the cost of 're'; re-doing, re-working, re-trying." And like insurance, not only does one shop around for coverage, but for cost.

> *"If you talk to a man in a language he understands, that goes to his head. If you talk to him in his language, that goes to his heart."*
>
> – NELSON MANDELA

"Leaders value advice based on how much they pay for it," Dan half-joked when discussing why it is so important for leaders to play an active, visual role in any transformation. Executives will engage sooner and more wholly when they know the risk impact of each change and how these actions affect their bottom line. Research reveals that with change management, if applied effectively, projects are 6 times more likely to finish on time and on budget with the actual desired product than those who do not leverage a formal CM methodology (Figure 3.0).

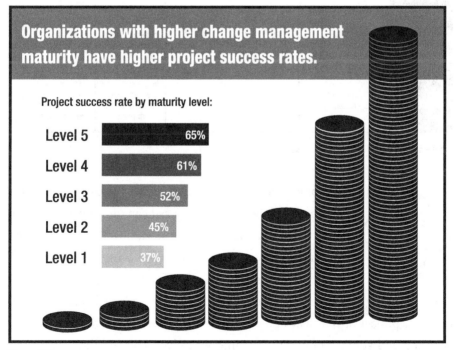

Organizations with higher change management maturity have higher project success rates.

Project success rate by maturity level:

Level 5	65%
Level 4	61%
Level 3	52%
Level 2	45%
Level 1	37%

Figure 3.0

Centra Health had the right idea in assessing their foundation prior to beginning their transformation. By evaluating their readiness, they learned where their strengths and weaknesses were so they could accurately address them and proceed in the best manner. Similar to the Gartner Maturity Matrix that Centra was ranked on, Prosci has a Maturity Model and audit tool that helps organizations do exactly this, breaking down by aspect – standardization, socialization, leadership, capabilities, etc. – where they are falling short (Figure 4.0).

Level 5	Organizational Competency	Change management competency is evident in all levels of the organization and is part of the organization's intellectual property and competitive edge	Continuous process improvement in place	Highest profitability and responsiveness
Level 4	Organizational Competency	Organization-wide standards and methods are broadly deployed for managing and leading change	Selection of common approach	
Level 3	Multiple Projects	Comprehensive apporach for managing change is being applied in multiple projects	Examples of best practices evident	
Level 2	Isolated Projectss	Some elements of change management are being applied in isolated projects	Many different tactics used inconsistently	
Level 1	Ad Hoc or Absent	Little or no change management applied	People-dependent without any formal practices or plans	Highest rate of project failure, turnover and productivity loss

Figure 4.0 – *Prosci, Inc. Change Management Maturity Model*

 The practices and techniques that stick around and aren't the flavors of the month, such as Lean, do so because their methodology truly works. At the earliest stage, an organization should engage in a formal process for change and build awareness for the transformation. Similarly to an Agile adoption, implementing a few CM techniques on a high profile, short duration project at first will quickly demonstrate its effectiveness, retain the attention and support of executives, and be easily referenced throughout the

enterprise. Over time, they will build up a CM muscle. Both Prosci and Lead-Quest agree the focus must be on "Progress, not perfection."

It seems that progress can only truly be made when the whole team is actively participating. We have stated repeatedly that executives must be active in a transformation. However, this may be counter-intuitive since many are in their position due to their ability to delegate. Executives may show their support and participation in regularly held meetings. In between those, the team is empowered to lead the initiative, but will often still look for approval and guidance, which is a normal phenomenon. "In an organization, the middle tends to look to the top for this while the bottom looks to the middle," explained Mark Sasscer of LeadQuest. This reinforces the roles that both executives and managers play in a transformation and how their participation impacts the attitude, motivation, and desire of the rest of the team. Bottom line is that their involvement and presence are vital to the process.

Backed by much research, it is not speculation that executive leaders have the most impact on a transformation; therefore, they must work to be the best

---

The 10 Principles of Personal Leadership
A Commitment to Continuous Improvement

1. Be in The Moment
2. Be Authentic & Humanistic
3. Volunteer Discretionary Effort Constantly
4. Model High Performance - Desired Behaviors that Drive Desired Results
5. Respect & Leverage Separate Realities
6. Be Curious vs. Judgmental
7. Look in the Mirror First - Be Accountable
8. Have Courageous Conversations
9. Provide Timely, Clear & Specific Performance Expectations & Feedback
10. Teach, Coach & Mentor - Spend at Least Half of Your Time Developing Others

---

Remember, "It's about progress, not perfection!"

Figure 5.0 | *LeadQuest Consulting, Inc.'s 10 Principles of Personal Leadership*

leaders they can during the transformation. LeadQuest developed *10 Principles of Personal Leadership* focused on a "Commitment to Continuous Improvement" (Figure 5.0).The slogan, itself, is Agile by definition.

People tend to confuse the role of leadership and management. Management is basically getting people to do what you want them to do whereas leadership is empowering others to participate. One of the 10 principles, and a central focus of any change management training or coaching, is accountability. This is a very appropriate point of emphasis when discussing leadership involvement.

Executives who are serious about ensuring the success of the transformation need to take high-profile actions that demonstrate their commitment to everyone. Executive action, like being present for the Centra Daily Stand-up and changing the format of the Parkview LDI meeting to include EPIC, gives unmistakable credibility and undeniable power to the transformation. It makes it clear that this is not just "the flavor of the month" soon to be forgotten. It fuels the change agents and unleashes the forces that can and will change the culture. One simply cannot expect a team to exhibit the desired behaviors without doing the same! And even if a leader is displaying this behavior, they must be visible for the team to see! After all, monkey-see, monkey-do!

Vendor Integration

Another core takeaway expressed in vastly different ways was vendor integration. Parkview's process for identifying a vendor and eliminating every possible aspect of wasted time looked, at first glance, like it was depreciating the unique potential and value of the individual suppliers. In reality it quickly got them to the brass tacks of forming an unbreakable, unambiguous relationship that would be durable enough to push through the unavoidable challenges that occur in every transformational change.

By instinctively applying the Lean principle of eliminating waste, Parkview's focus demonstrated respect for the resource cost suffered by potential partners during the sales cycle and also for the time of their own people. It minimized the waste for vendors and Parkview, as a whole, while optimizing the resource investment for the selected partner and Parkview. Colocating the decision-makers and legal teams in a single, uninterrupted 3-day session to resolve contract details, terms, and conditions was an amazing example of Agile-by-accident.

 Agile uses the term Spike to describe efforts that are short, high-intensity experiments to determine if a problem can be solved or an obstacle overcome. Parkview's approach was a spike to determine whether the vendor culture and approach was compatible with Parkview's needs for a revolutionary transformation. The result was a highly visible commitment from both organizations that the program was going to be a committed relationship and an integrated team.

Centra's expression of commitment to vendor integration occurred at a point in the project where the process of disintegration and failure begins. At the core of Centra's system transformation was the Cerner Revenue Cycle comprised of 6 projects. Its direct relationship to revenue and sustaining organizational metabolism made it vital. It was only 32% built when Jeff, Brian and the TMPMO were called upon to get involved and make things happen.

At the point when a project is failing, the most common reaction is finger-pointing, threats or lawsuits, but Jeff chose the more difficult path of real leadership. He decided that Cerner was a partner not just a vendor, and that they had to be integrated into any process that could create a path forward to the solution. Cerner and Centra had to act as an integrated whole but, as Jeff admits, that first month the meetings were rough as the standard for transparency and rigorous honesty was established. Jeff's commitment to "put everything on the table" and require complete, transparent communication meant facing Centra's failures and addressing Cerner's shortcomings in a way that was mutually respectful in the pursuit of realistic progress. Together they narrowed the focus to understanding how far behind they were and achieving each iteration goal. The result was a big win for the Revenue Cycle program as it hit over 90% built in just about 90 days. The increased progress was a direct result of the decision to integrate the vendor and create a partner relationship...with the help of Agile by design.

 Standard organizational charts show a structure that looks like tree roots with an implied top down fractal, suggesting that is how power is controlled and decisions manifest themselves. Such structures work well enough in enviroments that have a reasonable equilibrium, but fail miserably in situations that are not static. For industries, like healthcare, where a state of disequilibrium, complexity and uncertainty are the norm, using a network-based analogy to understand the dynamics of the ecosystem and aligning the variables for success has a higher probability of being right because the need for *ongoing transformation* is the only *constant.*

 Competent vendors must be integrated as trusted advisors in order for the organization to access the right insights at the right time, and be able to respond to them in the right way as only partners can do. Keeping an old paradigm where vendors are held at arm's length and distrusted ruptures the opportunity for the application of innovative ideas to systematically solve new and emerging threats and constraints. It is important to improve efficiency of production and minimize operational costs, but it is vital to unlock innovation to capitalize effectivity and triumph with real economies of scale. Companies must use vendor expertise to create systemic approaches that use a distributed decision-making model to deliver power at the point in their organizational structures where action must meet challenges. Successful companies take healthy advantage of the innovative benefits of social interactions to empower agents of change to overcome inefficiencies and delivery meaningful care.

Transparent Reporting

Within a given industry segment, companies tend to be approximately similar using versions of core practices, such as Generally Accepted Accounting Practices (GAAP) or, in the healthcare industry, the International Statistical Classification of Diseases and Related Health Problems (ICD-10) and EHR systems. But the idea that Wal-Mart ($353 billion, 2016) is an approximately scaled up version of a smaller, modest-sized Sears ($22 billion, 2016) only applies to the practices, processes and systems that don't impact strategic marketplace advantage. Factors that drive strategic differentiation and marketplace advantage, whether it is pricing models and logistics execution in the retail industry, or patient care, regulatory compliance and billing efficiency in healthcare, are the 20% that drives 80% of the impact expressed in the Pareto principle.

 Transparent reporting on actual progress being made, and learning and discovery in real-time, gives executives the information they need to make timely adjustments that deliver desired outcomes. *Enterprise agility has a much broader scope that is more important than Agile project management, but Agile project management is a key enabler of enterprise agility.* Project management and project execution have become vital, strategic enablers precisely because they focus critical resources on making meaningful change with acceptable speed.

Meaningful change with acceptable speed is a good definition of pragmatic innovation and enterprise agility. Such agility helps ensure the organization's long-term future by allowing it to respond effectively to the ever more diverse spectrum of activities required by incessantly changing customer expectations and expanding regulation.

Likewise, transparent reporting on progress without clear, well-designed metrics nearly guarantees the sub-optimization of critical parts of the organization, moving the transformation from hard to very hard or even impossible. And metrics, even well-designed metrics, not supported by effective, efficient progress-oriented reporting causes inaction and paralysis. Poorly designed metrics can create competition within the leadership ranks and divide the focus instead of unifying it.

Both Centra and Parkview succeeded because they cultivated a culture that respects and values honest, accurate, transparent reporting where every participant experienced the Agile norm of 'personal safety' when undesirable results had to be shared. Whether executives invest themselves in making personal safety and transparent reporting the two sides of the 'coin of the realm' strongly correlates to the probability of success achieving enterprise agility.

Pitfall Avoided

 Driving enterprise agility begins with transparent reporting based on estimates that support effective decision-making, yet many executives accidentally or unknowingly sow the seeds of failure by communicating the perception they require detailed long-term estimates. Creating or accepting a standard where the metrics for estimates are detailed and long-term is a mistake. It is mathematically impossible in the real world of strategic differentiation and marketplace advantage to have both of those variables simultaneously. Pursuing or expecting it drives up costs and drives down effective decision-making.

For the organizational activities that require learning and discovery to achieve pragmatic innovation and enterprise agility there is an unavoidable, non-linear distortion caused by both time and size, often referred to in Agile as the Cone of Uncertainty. That does not mean that valuable, useful estimates cannot be made. It does mean that articulating an expectation that aligns the granularity of estimates with the granularity of decision-making is vitally important and must be driven by the executive leaders.

In every organizational context there are essentially three decision-making time horizons – near-term, mid-term and long-term. For a healthcare enterprise those thresholds might be 6 months, 1 year, and 3+ years, while in a website development business it might be 8 weeks, 16 weeks, and 9 months. In every case the size of the decisions being made get smaller and the details get more refined as they approach the near-term horizon. Decisions in the long-term range are large, broad stroke and directional while decisions in the near-term are small, detailed and precise, specifically because of the unavoidable distortion of time and size.

 Decisions farther out in time are subject to uncontrollable, and somewhat unknowable, marketplace forces and technological changes, to say nothing of stakeholder expectations. The amount of change that can occur over 3 years is not just three-times what can occur in 1 year; it is much more! The amount of change that can occur within a $30 million project in not just three-times what can occur in a $10 million project. It is much more. And that fact is like the law of gravity. You can't change it and you ignore it at your own peril!

When I raised this issue with Rick A. Morris, MPM, PMP, PMI-ACP, SCM and a respected veteran in the battles to achieve organizational agility, he said, "One important thing we've learned about enterprise agility is that many organizations make the mistake of committing to projects on an initiative by initiative by initiative basis and end up overloading their teams, thereby inducing risk and often causing failure."

He continued, "Almost every company in America has too many initiatives and not enough people. Their approach cultivates failure because they have no idea what the enterprise is actually working on. They don't have a comprehensive, cogent view of total resources across all projects and they seem to believe it is impossible to have one. They just keep approving new initiatives without understanding what it is doing to their teams, their projects and their portfolios. They don't understand they are harming operating results.

We discovered that when our clients really started to look at making Agile seriously productive, they looked at funding processes and linked them to project and portfolio management. Honestly, it is a little frustrating that so many companies don't realize how easily this can be accomplished. And, of course, it is immensely satisfying for us to help clients identify that teams are only a point, a resource, that can be managed, despite some struggles, but when they start to reverse that prior negative flow, the results are amazing."

Essentially, executives can enable agility just by realizing and articulating that a group of people – a team – can be funded for a certain period of time to work in alignment with these development outcomes defined at certain levels of granularity. Whether you use Traditional or Agile terms, call them Iterations Goals or Milestones, development outcomes must become the focus of where teams start looking to see what the maximum is that they can realistically produce.

The truth is that the cost of the team is fairly consistent over time and the only real variable is the number of features, functions or capabilities that that team can produce. Managing and defining funding at the team level provides the team some stability so that they can continue forward movement producing value. The impact of that choice is that your teams become focused on producing value and focused on really moving the next best function forward.

Proper granularity in strategic planning drives proper granularity in estimating, which then powers up a system where program or project backlogs are intelligent and transparent enough that self-organizing teams operate with autonomy at the Iteration and Milestone decision-making level. Those teams interlink with self-directing teams then operate with autonomy at the Release and Project decision-making level. And, ultimately, those teams integrate with self-managing teams that operate with autonomy at the Roadmap and Program/Portfolio decision-making level.

Rick summarized by saying, "Properly structured decision-making means that planning, estimating, funding and accounting functions auto-magically integrate within a properly configured technology system and produce transparent reporting that feeds cogent information back into planning. That results in executives having better information to make better decisions that drive better operating results."

Proper granularity defines the variables so a properly configured technology system becomes a major contributor to operational success by reducing the cost of rework and poor quality and lowering the overhead of managing and leading the organization.

Embracing that fact opens the door to using approaches that are more cost effective and lead to better outcomes because they align estimating, decision-making and the Cone of Uncertainty. Executive's must understand and then effectively articulate a standard that aligns the perspective being used for decision-making with the processes being used for estimating. A good lexicon for doing so is Definitive, Budgetary and Rough-order-of-Magnitude (ROM) for near-, mid- and long-term estimates.

Definitive estimates are much more expensive because they require the acquisition, analysis and application of much more information which requires time, usually from expensive engineers or technical professionals. But the cost is typically justified on a 90-day or, perhaps, 6-month horizon because it directly impacts staffing, funding and other critical decisions.

By comparison, very effective and efficient Budgetary decision-making can occur on the mid-term horizon using much less granular, less expensive information by applying an approach, such as Planning Poker, that systematically incorporates a Fibonacci-type, non-linear number series and comparative assessment of size and complexity.

Lastly, strategically effective long-term decision-making can be done at the ROM level of granularity because the decisions are, by definition, large, broad stroke and directional. As John Maynard Keynes, the well-known economist, said, "It is better to be roughly right than precisely wrong." Being in the right market, with the right capabilities at the right time does not require an exact, detailed list of the products features or costs. It does require the competency to make meaningful change with acceptable speed in the direction of pragmatic innovation and enterprise agility! Such estimates can be accomplished using an approach such as Affinity estimating that also employs a comparative assessment of size and complexity.

Leaders need to articulate Defined Granularity standards in order to leverage the power of Definitive, Budgetary and ROM/Strategic decision-making and unleash organizational innovation, differentiation, or profitability.

Conclusion

caling Agile has great potential, as an agent-based model, to unleash the innovative potential of the whole organization to define and leverage a framework that addresses the big issues challenging survival in healthcare – both for the patients and the organization. To access that opportunity, executives must consider the entire system as an integrated whole with the capacity to be more than the sum of its idealized bits and pieces. They must recognize that the marketplace is not in a state of equilibrium, and never will be again, so future success can only be achieved with an evolving enterprise whose systems embed emergent properties and optimize the underlying interactions between all the actors. That means a crucial requirement is the specification of the rules for decision-making, and those rules must support the experience, intuition and insight of everyone in the practitioner environment so that critical information, fundamental principles and meaningful use are optimized as a whole.

As both Centra and Parkview have demonstrated, Agile can deliver success in the midst of nearly overwhelming challenges when creative insights unbridle organizational structures and unleash personal empowerment in a systemic way.

Useful Resources

●●

Am I Agile Already? - Quiz

"Select the Option that BEST describes your organization"

1. I regularly hold status meetings with all team members in attendance.
    - ○ Never
    - ○ Occasionally, if there are issues to address
    - ○ Usually, unless something prevents it
    - ○ Always

2. During the initial phase of a project, our organization understands that detailed budget estimates are unreliable.
    - ○ Never
    - ○ Occasionally, if denial is unavoidable
    - ○ Usually, but they still want a budget
    - ○ Always

3. Team members are encouraged to share feedback on progress and also needs from other team members, managers or executives.
    - ○ Never
    - ○ Occasionally. Team members speak with the team leaders who communicate feedback outside the team.
    - ○ Usually, but sometimes team members feel 'at risk' when sharing needs or challenges
    - ○ Always

4. Our organization and PMO support the use of processes tailored to the needs of each project.
   - ○ Never
   - ○ Occasionally, in exceptional cases
   - ○ Usually, but depends on the Project Manager
   - ○ Always

5. At any given time, team members know the status of the project and who is working on what and why.
   - ○ Never
   - ○ Occasionally. Team leaders know the status and they manage the flow of information to the team.
   - ○ Usually
   - ○ Always

6. If the team runs into an obstacle, they have quick, easy access to someone to remove it.
   - ○ Never
   - ○ Occasionally, as soon as the correct committee or person can be notified
   - ○ Usually, unless it is a very rare situation
   - ○ Always

7. Management accepts responsibility if the team fails due to factors beyond their control.
   - ○ Never
   - ○ Occasionally, if the team can prove a documented request for help with a consequential warning
   - ○ Usually, except when the team refused to follow the agreed upon path to prevent failure
   - ○ Always

8. When I assign development projects, I trust the team to complete them and avoid micro-managing them.
   - ○ Never
   - ○ Occasionally, because they need to be managed
   - ○ Usually, with experienced teams
   - ○ Always

9. Team members feel safe sharing 'constructive criticism' and perceived risks or challenges that may impact project success regardless of the 'rank' of the person implicated or source of the problem.
   - ○ Never
   - ○ Occasionally, if they can document their observations convincingly
   - ○ Usually, especially once they get aligned to our culture
   - ○ Always

10. As much as possible, our culture is to keep team members together as a unit as they transition from one project to the next in order to benefit from their team maturity.
    - ○ Never
    - ○ Occasionally, but not by design
    - ○ Usually, but it is not always possible
    - ○ Always

If you selected Usually or Always:

1-3 times then…. *You have not started being Agile already.*

4-7 times then…. *You are more Agile already than you may realize.*

8-10 times then… *You are definitely Agile already.*

Additional Resources

➤ DistilledInsight.com

➤ The Agile Almanac – Books 1 and 2 by John Stenbeck

➤ GR8PM.com

➤ Prosci.com

➤ Accountability Now! by Mark Sasscer

About the Authors

● ●

JOHN G. STENBECK, PMP, PMI-ACP, CSM, CSP, ITIL, is the Founder of GR8PM, Inc. (pronounced "Great PM"). John is a three-time *Amazon #1 Best Selling* author. His industry-leading project management books have reached almost $3 million in sales. His books include the *Agile Almanac Book 1* and *Book 2* (with *Book 3* of the trilogy due in 2019), *Agile Government Contracting, The Professional Project Manager's Guide to Understanding Agile in the PMBOK® Guide Sixth Edition and the Agile Practice Guide* and this book, *Enterprise Agility in Healthcare (part of the Distilled Insight series),* which is highly anticipated to join his list of Amazon #1 Best Sellers upon release.

He has been a guest on VoiceAmerica talk radio, Good Morning America, the Today Show, Fox News and the Oprah Winfrey Show. John has been featured on the front page of the Los Angeles Times and the San Diego Union.

John is a sought-after Keynote speaker because he enables executives and technical professionals to become *powerfully productive leaders!*

A partial list of John's clients includes: Booz Allen Hamilton, Inc., McLean, VA; County of Orange, Orange, CA; Hewlett-Packard Company, Palo Alto, CA; Lucent Technologies, Allentown, PA; Nike Corp., Beaverton, OR; Oracle Corp., Redwood Shores, CA; Qualcomm, Inc., San Diego, CA; U.S. Army – Space and Terrestrial Communications Directorate, Fort Monmouth, NJ; U.S.D.A. – National Finance Center, New Orleans, LA; U.S. Marine Corp. Systems Command, Stafford, VA; Visa – Smart Cards, Foster City, CA.

Villanova University's online certificate programs include 71 video lectures recorded for them by John. He has taught numerous public and corporate on-site programs to over 15,000 participants. John helps technical professionals master project management and leadership skills dramatically improving their contribution to enterprise results.

John holds PMI's Project Management Professional (PMP®) credential and Agile Certified Practitioner (PMI-ACP®) certification. He also holds Certified Scrum Master (CSM) and Certified Scrum Professional (CSP) designations from the Scrum Alliance and an ITIL v3 Foundations certification.

● ●

LAUREN E. MIX, EDITOR IN CHIEF/OWNER OF LM EDITING, whether in the role of editor, ghostwriter, or co-author, has a unique background that makes her a valuable asset to technically sophisticated books.

When editing, she works on selected projects where her background provides more than just proofreading. The manuscripts she edits involve collaborations where her value as a neutral and independent expert adds to the competence of the author, assisting in the struggle to find the clearest, most accessible way to create maximum knowledge transfer for the reader. Lauren's career experience allows her to add insight to existing content and expand it to reach the full potential audience. Because she goes beyond mere copyediting and understands the technical jargon of the content, she is able to compile a comprehensive index and glossary with less guidance from authors than other editors, giving authors more time to focus on their tasks.

Lauren has also taken on the additional role of ghost-writer where she has either contributed valuable input to an author's content, expanding on their existing concepts with her knowledge of the subject, or turned thought patterns and ideas into comprehensive text, targeted at the specific audience desired.

Recently, Lauren has added the role of co-author to her resume. She created Distilled Insight, a series that focuses on bringing specific knowledge points to executives in a fast-paced, high-value manner to expedite content comprehension and application. In addition to being the lead author, she has also developed the structure of the books, arranged and organized the content, and worked closely with graphic design on the contained images and with the publisher to ensure on-time completion.

Lauren is a very focused, driven individual who does not shy away from any challenge. She relishes opportunities to learn new skills then hones them to increase her value in the field. With exceptionally strong organizational skills and self-discipline, Lauren is able to manage multiple projects simultaneously with ease.

A sample of texts Lauren has edited includes:

John G. Stenbeck's:

- *Agile Almanac – Book 1*
- *Agile Almanac – Book 2 (ghostwrote as well)*
- *The Professional Project Manager's Guide to the PMBOK Guide, Sixth Edition*
- *PMI Agile Certified Practitioner (ACP®) Exam Preparation*
- *Agile Almanac: Desk Reference and PM Field Guide*
- *Agile Government Contracting*
- *The Professional Project Manager's Guide to PMBOK 6*

And:

- *No Day But Today* by Rick Morris
- *Scrum For the Rest of Us* by Brian Rabon
- *Ripen* by Jeff Graddy and Sacha Lindekens
- *Sit Be Fit* by Joana Brown
- *Peak Performance CEO* by Joana Brown

In addition to her manuscript functions, Lauren has over a decade of experience in the Oil and Gas, Energy, and Chemical industries in various roles, including Technical Project Manager, Director of Business Development, and Senior Project Coordinator. Over the past 8 years she has mainly consulted with clients in Energy, assisting them with performance analysis, maintenance trending and root-cause analysis, and budget and execution process streamlining. She has almost a decade of experience working with a variety of energy facilities, including renewable fuel cells, combined cycle/natural gas, coal, and LNG distribution.

A sample of clients Lauren has worked with includes: Dominion Energy, Duke Energy, Fuel Cell Energy, DuPont Chemical, NuStar Refining, Valero, Sunoco Logistics, and Colonial Pipeline.

She has been a member of the Project Management Institute (PMI®) and attends pertinent conferences in her industry regularly.

In her "spare" time, she enjoys caring for and playing with her animals on her farm in New England.

Lauren Mix, Editor in Chief/Owner
LM Editing
(603) 660-9090 Cell
(603) 529-0368 Office
LMEditservices@gmail.com
www.LMEditingservices.com

LM Editing

Index